The Poetry of Laurence Binyon

Volume IV - Odes

Robert Laurence Binyon, CH, was born on August 10th, 1869 in Lancaster in Lancashire, England to Quaker parents, Frederick Binyon and Mary Dockray.

He studied at St Paul's School, London before enrolling at Trinity College, Oxford, to read classics.

Binyon's first published work was Persephone in 1890. As a poet, his output was not prodigious and, in the main, the volumes he did publish were slim. But his reputation was of the highest order. When the Poet Laureate, Alfred Austin, died in 1913, Binyon was considered alongside Thomas Hardy and Rudyard Kipling for the post which was given to Robert Bridges.

Binyon played a pivotal role in helping to establish the modernist School of poetry and introduced imagist poets such as Ezra Pound, Richard Aldington and H.D. (Hilda Doolittle) to East Asian visual art and literature. Most of his career was spent at The British Museum where he produced many books particularly centering on the art of the Far East.

Moved and shaken by the onset of the World War I and its military tactics of young men slaughtered to hold or gain a few yards of shell-shocked mud Binyon wrote his seminal poem *For the Fallen*. It became an instant classic, turning moments of great loss into a National and human tribute.

After the war, he returned to the British Museum and wrote numerous books on art; especially on William Blake, Persian and Japanese art.

In 1931, his two volume Collected Poems appeared and in 1933, he retired from the British Museum.

Between 1933 and 1943, Binyon published his acclaimed translation of Dante's *Divine Comedy* in an English version of terza rima.

During the Second World War Binyon wrote another poetic masterpiece *'The Burning of the Leaves'*, about the London Blitz.

Robert Laurence Binyon died in Dunedin Nursing Home, Bath Road, Reading, on March 10th, 1943 after undergoing an operation.

Index of Contents

ODES

THE DRYAD

What hath the ilex heard,
What hath the laurel seen,
That the pale edges of their leaves are stirred?
What spirit stole between?
O trees upon your circle of smooth green,
You stir as youths when beauty paces by.
Moving heart and eye
To unuttered praise.
Was it the wind that parted your light boughs.
Some odour to recapture as he strays,
Or some fair virgin shape of human brows
Yet lost to human gaze?

O for that morning of the simple world,
When hollow oak and fount and flowering reed
Were storied each with glimpses of a face
By dropping hair dew-pearled!
Strange eyes that had no heed
Of men, and bodies shy with the firm grace
Of young fawns flying, yet of human kin,
Whose hand might lead us, could we only spare
Doubt and suspicious pride, a world to win,
Where all that lives would speak with us, now dumb
For fear of us. O might I yet win there!
Wave, boughs, aside! to your fresh glooms I come.

But all is lonely here!
Yet lonelier is the glade
Than the wood's entrance, and more dark appear
The hollows of still shade.
Ah, yet the nymph's white feet have surely stayed
Beside the spring; how solitary fair
Shines and trembles there
White narcissus bloom!
By lichened gray stones, where the glancing stream
Swerves over into green wet mossy gloom,
Their snowy frail flames on the ripple gleam
And all the place illume.

Surely her feet a moment rested here!
Nerving her hand upon a pliant branch,
She paused, she listened, and then glided on
Half-turned in lovely fear;
And her young shoulder shone
Like moonbeams that wet sands, foam-bordered, blanch,
A sight to stay the beating of the breast!
Alas, but mortal eyes may never know
That beauty. Hark, what bird above his nest
So rapturously sings? Ah, thou wilt tell.
Thou perfect flower, whither her footsteps go.
And all her thoughts, pure flower, for thou know'st well.

White sweetness, richest odours round thee cling.
Purely thou breathest of voluptuous Spring!
Thou art so white, because thou dost enclose
All the advancing splendours of the year;
And thou hast burned beyond the reddest rose,
To shine so keenly clear.
Shadowed within thy radiance I divine
Frail coral tinges of the anemone.
Dim blue that clouds upon the columbine.
And wallflower's glow as of old, fragrant wine.
And the first tulip's sanguine clarity,
And pansy's midnight-purple of sole star!
All these that wander far
From thee, and wilder glories would assume,
Ev'n the proud peony of drooping plume,
Robed like a queen in Tyre,
All to thy lost intensity aspire;
Toward thee they yearn out of encroaching gloom;
They are all faltering beams of thy most perfect fire!

And she, that only haunts remote green ways.
Is it an empty freedom she doth praise?
Doth she, distrustfully averse, despise
The common sweet of passion, apt to fault?
And turns she from the hunger in love's eyes
Pale famine to exalt?
Oh no, her bosom's maiden hope is still
A morning dewdrop, imaging complete
All life, full-stored with every generous thrill;
No hope less perfect could her body fill,
Nor she be false to her own heart's rich beat.
But she is pure because she hath not soiled
Hope with endeavour foiled;
She not condemns glad love, but with the best

Enshrines it, lovelier because unpossest.
Where is the joy we meant
In our first love, the joy so swiftly spent?
It glows for ever in her sacred breast,
Untamed to languor's ebb, nor by hot passion rent.

O pure abstaining Priestess of delight,
That treasurest apart love's sanctity.
Art thou but vision of an antique dream,
Mated with a song's flight.
With beckoning western gleam
Or first rose fading from an early sky?
Yet we, that are of earth, must seek on earth
Our bodied bliss. Nay, thou hast still thine hour;
And in a girl's life-trusting April mirth,
Or noble boy's clear and victorious eyes,
Thou shinest with the charm and with the power
Of all that wisdom loses to be wise.

THE BACCHANAL OF ALEXANDER

'Alexander, returning from his Indian Conquests, having with infinite difficulty brought his army through the salt deserts of Gedrosia, arrived in the pleasant country of the Carmanians, Some authors tell us, that reclining with his friends upon two chariots chained together, and having his ears entertained by the most delicious music, he led his army through Carmania, the soldiers following him with dances and garlands, in emulation of the ancient Bacchanals of Dionysus." — Arrian.

I

A wondrous rumour fills and stirs
The wide Carmanian Vale;
On leafy hills the sunburnt vintagers
Stand listening; silent is the echoing flail
Upon the threshing-floors:
Girls in the orchards one another hail
Over their golden stores.
"Leave the dewy apples hanging flushed,
Ripe to drop
In our baskets! Leave the heavy grapes un crushed,
Leave the darkened figs, a half-pulled crop,
Olive-boughs by staves unbeaten, come.
All our hills be hushed!
For a Conqueror, nay a God,
Comes into our land this day.
From the Eastern desert dumb,
That no mortal ever trod:

Come we down to meet him on his way!"

From reddening vineyards steeped in sun.
Trees that with riches droop,
Down the green upland men and maidens run
Or under the low leaves with laughter stoop.
But now they pause, they hear
Far trampling sounds; and many a soft-eyed troop
Murmurs a wondering fear.
"Wherefore hast thou summoned us afar,
Voice so proud?
Who are ye that so imperious are?
Is it he to whom all India bowed,
Bacchus, and the great host that pursue
Triumphing, his car;
Whom our fathers long foretold?
O if it be he, the God indeed,
May his power our vines endue
With prosperity fourfold.
Bring we all ripe offerings for his need!"

Slowly along the vine-robed vale move on,
Like those that walk in dream,
The ranks of Macedon.
O much-proved men, why doubt ye truth so sweet?
This is that fair Carmania, that did seem
So far to gain, yet now is at your feet.
'Tis no Circean magic greenly crowds
This vale of elms, the laden vines uprearing,
The small flowers in the grass, the illumined clouds.
Trembling streams with rushes lined.
All in strangeness reappearing
Like a blue morn to the blind!
Worn feet go happy, and parched throats may laugh,
Or blissful cold drops from dipt helmets quaff;
Dear comrades, flinging spears down, stand embraced
And heap this rich oblivion on the waste
Of torment whence they came;
That land of salt sand vaulted o'er with flame,
That furnace, which for sixty days they pierced.
Wrapt in a hot slow cloud of pricking grains,
On ever crumbling mounds, through endless plains.
And ravening hands scooped fire, not water, for their thirst.
Streams of Carmania, never have ye seen
Such mirrored rapture of strong limbs unclad.
Lips pressing, lover-like, delicious green
Of leaves, or breaking into laughter mad;
Out-wearied ranks, that couched in gloom serene.

Let idle memory toy
With torment past whose pangs enrich the gust of joy.

II

O peerless Alexander! Still
From his kindling words they glow.
Like a straight shaft to a bow
Is their strength unto his will.
He hath done what no man ever dared:
That fierce desert, where great Cyrus lost,
All save seven of his unnumbered host.
Where the proud Semiramis despaired.
He hath brought his thousands through.
Vainly, vainly Wind and Fire
Stormed against the way of his desire:
They at last their tamer knew.
O'er mile-broad rivers, like young brooks, he stept.
Walls of unconquered cities overle'pt.
And now Earth yields, for storm and strife and heat.
Her greenest valley to his feet.

But lo! the soft Carmanian folk,
Round these warriors gathering nigh,
Down the slopes with murmur shy
The benignant God invoke.
While they stand in wonder and in doubt,
Comes a throng in leaves their heads arraying.
Some on pipes and some on tabors playing,
"Bacchus, Bacchus is our king," they shout,
"Magic mirth into our blood he pours;
Join us, strangers, in our feast!
All our parching toil hath ceased.
Give us of your fruitful valley's stores!"
Apples they heap on shields in golden domes,
And spearpoints bear the dripping honeycombs.
"Our Bacchus bids you to his joy," they sing;
"Lo, where he comes, the king!"

Two massy ivory cars, together bound.
Roll through the parting throng;
A whole uprooted vine enwreathes them round;
Long tendrils over the gold axles trail,
While jubilant pipe and chanted song
The cars' oncoming hail.
By the dark bunches idle helms and greaves
Are hung, and swords that on Hydaspes shone;

Heroic shoulders gleam betwixt the leaves!
There sits reclined on rugs of Susa spread,
Throned amid his Seven of Macedon,
Alexander! his victorious head
Bound with ivy and pale autumn flowers.
Ah, what a sunny redolence of showers
The wind wafts round him from this promised land!
Over Hephaestion's neck is laid one hand,
Lightly the other holds a spear; but now
No passion fires his eye, nor deep thought knots his brow.
Like his own Pella breathes this upland air;
A joy-born beauty flushes up his face,
O'ersmoothing old fell rages, to replace
Youth in lost lines most indolently fair.
Remembrance is at peace, desire forgone,
And those winged brows their watchful menace ease
In languor proud as a storm-sailing swan
New lighted on a mere from the wild seas.
Beat, thrilling drums, beat low, and pipes sound on,
While his full soul doth gaze
From this the topmost hour of all his glorious days.

III

The shy Carmanians awed
Gaze on that sun-like head.
"Is it he," they murmur, "who led
The mirth of the vineyard abroad?
Surely none else may bear
So regal a beauty; yet why
On us turns not his eye?
We have heard that he loves not care.
But the dance and idle glee
Of the laughing Satyr tribe.
Could toil those brows inscribe?
Is it he? is it surely he?
Are these the revellers of his train?
Yet surely these have passed through fire, through pain!
Can the Gods also suffer throes,
Nor crave to conquer, but repose?"
The king uplifts his bowl.
Peucestas stoops, pours in
From a brown fawn's swelling skin
The ripe grape's rosy soul.
"Pledge us," he cries, and smiles,
"Lord of Nysa, to-day!
Have we not toiled our way

To a valley of the Blessed Isles?
Drink of a richer boon
Than the water we brought thee to taste
In the fiery Gedrosian waste
When we halted our host at noon,
And thou in the sight of all didst spill
Those longed-for drops on the darkened sand, — O fill.
Remembering how our hearts drank wine
From thy refusing deed divine."

What hath the king so stirred?
What grief of a great desire
Stung by that spoken word?
Sudden as storm his thoughts tumultuous run
Back into peril, Indus, Issus, Tyre,
And the famed gates of Babylon yet unwon.
Far, far those mighty days in glory tower!
A valley keeps him, while the great peaks call.
O for that supreme exultant hour,
When alone, Achilles-like, he sprang
'Mid the astonished Indians o'er the wall.
And a hundred arrows round him rang!
O Alexander, all these thousands own
Thy pleasure, but thy throes were thine alone.
Dulled is the joy that hath no need to dare;
Match thy great self, and breed another heir
To those high deeds, from which thy kindled fame
Runs, as the world's hope runs from youth to youth aflame.
Climb, climb again to those lone eagle skies.
Where Ocean's unadventured circle bends
And dragon ignorance girdles the world's ends! —
As fire leaps up a tower, that thought leaps to his eyes.
"Off, Maenad mummery," he cries; his brow
Strips of its garland with indignant hands.
Starts up, and plants his ringing spear; and now
Soul-flushed through radiant limbs, a man transfigured stands.
With joy the marvelling Carmanians bow.
From their long doubting freed:
"It is the God," they cry, "the enraptured God indeed!"

ASOKA

I

Gentle as fine rain falling from the night,
The first beams from the Indian moon at full

Steal through the boughs, and brighter and more bright
Glide like a breath, a fragrance visible.
Asoka round him sees
The gloom ebb into glories half-espied
Of glimmering bowers through wavering traceries:
Pale as a rose by magical degrees
Opening, the air breaks into beauty wide,
And yields a mystic sweet;
And shapes of leaves shadow the pathway side
Around Asoka's feet.
O happy prince! From his own court he steals;
Weary of words is he, weary of throngs.
How this wide ecstasy of stillness heals
His heart of flatteries and the tale of wrongs!
Unseen he climbs the hill,
Unheard he brushes with his cloak the dew,
While the young moonbeams every hollow fill
With hovering flowers, so gradual and so still
As though from growing joy the radiance grew.
Discovering pale gold
Of spikenard balls and champak buds that new
Upon the air unfold.
He gains the ridge. Wide open rolls the night!
Airs from an infinite horizon blow
Down holy Ganges, floating vast and bright
Through old Magadha's forests. Far below
He hears the cool wave fret
On rocky islands; soft as moths asleep
Come moonlit sails; there on a parapet
Of ruined marble, where the moss gleams wet
And from black cedars a lone peacock cries.
Uncloaking rests Asoka, bathing deep
In silence, and his eyes
Of his own realm the wondrous prospect reap;
At last aloud he sighs.

II

"How ennobling it is to taste
Of the breath of a living power!
The shepherd boy on the waste
Whose converse, hour by hour,
Is alone with the stars and the sun,
His days are glorified!
And the steersman floating on
Down this great Ganges tide,
He is blest to be companion of the might

Of waters and unwearied winds that run
With him, by day, by night:
He knows not whence they come, but they his path provide.

"But O more noble far
From the heart of power to proceed
As the beam flows forth from the star,
As the flower unfolds on the reed.
It is not we that are strong
But the cause, the divine desire.
The longing wherewith we long.
O flame far-springing from the eternal fire.
Feed, feed upon my heart till thou consume
These bonds that do me wrong
Of time and chance and doom.
And I into thy radiance grow and glow entire!

"For he who his own strength trusts,
And by violence hungers to tame
Men and the earth to his lusts,
Though mighty, he falls in shame;
As a great fell tiger, whose sound
The small beasts quake to hear.
When he stretches his throat to the shuddering ground
And roars for blood; yet a trembling deer
Brings him at last to his end.
In a winter torrent falls his murderous bound!
His raging claws the unheeding waters rend;
Down crags they toss him sheer.
With sheep ignobly drowned.
And his fierce heart is burst with fury of its fear.

III

"Not so ye deal,
Immortal Powers, with him
Who in his weak hour hath made haste to kneel
Where your divine springs out of mystery brim,
And carries thence through the world's uproar rude
A clear-eyed fortitude;
As mid the blue noon on the Arabian strand
The solitary diver, plunging deep.
Glides down the rough dark brine with questing hand
Until he feels upleap
Founts of fresh water, and his goatskin swells
And bears him upward on those buoyant wells
Back with a cool boon for his thirsting land.

"I also thirst,
O living springs, for you:
Would that I might drink now, as when at first
Life shone about me glorious and all true,
And I abounded in your strength indeed.
Which now I sorely need.
You have not failed, 'tis I! Yet this abhorred
Necessity to hate and to despise —
'Twas not for this my youthful longing soared,
Not thus would I grow wise!
Keep my heart tender still, that still is set
To love without foreboding or regret,
Even as this tender moonlight is outpoured.

"Now now, even now.
Sleep doth the sad world take
To peace it knows not. Radiant Sleep, wilt thou
Unveil thy wonder for me too, who wake?
O my soul melts into immensity,
And yet 'tis I, 'tis I!
A wave upon a silent ocean, thrilled
Up from its deepest deeps without a sound,
Without a shore to break on, or a bound.
Until the world be filled.
O mystery of peace, O more profound
Than pain or joy, upbuoy me on thy power!
Stay, stay, adored hour,
I am lost, I am found again:
My soul is as a fountain springing in the rain."

— Long, long upon that cedarn-shadowed height
Musing, Asoka mingled with the night.
At last the moon sank o'er the forest wide.
Within his soul those fountains welled no more,
Yet breathed a balm still, fresh as fallen dew:
The mist coiled upward over Ganges shore;
And he arose and sighed.
And gathered his cloak round him, and anew
Threaded the deep woods to his palace door.

THE DEATH OF TRISTRAM

I

Tristram lies sick to death;

Dulled is his kingly eye,
Listless his famed right arm: earth-weary breath
Hath force alone to sigh
The one name that re-kindles life's low flame,
Isoult! — And thou, fair moon of Tristram's eve,
Who with that many-memoried name didst take
A glory for the sake
Of her who shone the sole light of his days and deeds.
Thou canst no more relieve
This heart that inly bleeds
With all thy love, with all thy tender lore,
No, nor thy white hands soothe him any more.
Still, the day-long, she hears
Kind words that are more sharp to her than spears.
Ah, loved he more, he had not been so kind!
And still with pricking tears
She watches him, and still must seem resigned;
Though well she knows what face his eyes require,
And jealous pangs, like coiled snakes in her mind,
Cling tighter, as that voice more earnestly
Asks heavy with desire
From out that passionate past which is not hers,
"Sweet wife, is there no sail upon the sea?"

Tenderest hearts by pain grow oft the bitterest,
And haste to wound the thing they love the best.
At evening, at sun-set, to Tristram's bed
News on her lip she brings!
She comes with eyes bright in divining dread,
Hardening her anguished heart she bends above his head.
"O Tristram!" — How her low voice strangely rings! —
"There comes a ship, ah, rise not, turn not pale.
I know not what this means, it is a sail
Black, black as night! " She shot her word, and fled.
But Tristram cried
With a great cry, and rose upon his side.
"It cannot be, it cannot, shall not be!
I will not die until mine own eyes see."
Despair, more strong than hope, lifts his weak limbs;
He stands and draws deep effort from his breath,
He trembles, his gaze swims,
He gropes his steps in pain,
Nigh fainting, till he gain
Salt air and brightness from the outer door
That opens on the cliff-built bastion floor
And the wide ocean gleaming far beneath.
He gazes, his lips part,
And all the blood pours back upon his heart.

Close thine eyes, Tristram, lest joy blind thee quite!
So swift a splendour burns away thy doubt.
Nay, Tristram, gaze, gaze, lest bright Truth go out
Ere she hath briefly shone.
White, dazzling white,
A sail swells onward, filling all his sight
With snowy light!
As on a gull's sure wing the ship comes on;
She towers upon the wave, she speeds for home.
Tristram on either doorpost must sustain
His arms for strength to gaze his fill again.
She shivers off the wind; the shining foam
Bursts from her pitching prow.
The sail drops as she nears,
Poised on the joyous swell; and Tristram sees
The mariners upon the deck; he hears
Their eager cries; the breeze
Blows a white cloak; and now
O'er all the rest, like magic in his ears,
A voice, that empties all the earth and sky,
Comes clear across the water, "It is I!"

Isoult is come! Victorious saints above,
Who suffered anguish ere to bliss you died,
Have pity on him whom Love so sore hath tried,
Who sinned yet greatly suffered for his love.
That dear renounced love when now he sees.
Heavy with joy, he sinks upon his knees.
O had she wings to lift her to his side!
But she is far below
Where the spray breaks upon the rusted rail
And rock-hewn steps, and there
Stands gazing up, and lo!
Tristram, how faint and pale!
A pity overcomes her like despair.
How shall her strength avail
To conquer that steep stair,
Dark, terrible, and ignorant as Time,
Up which her feet must climb
To Tristram? His outstretching arms are fain
To help her, yet are helpless; and his pain
Is hers, and her pain Tristram's; with long sighs
She mounts, then halts again.
Till she have drawn strength from his love-dimmed eyes:
But when that wasted face anew she sees,
Despair anew subdues her knees:
She fails, yet still she mounts by sad degrees.

With all her soul into her gaze upcast.
Until at last, at last . . .
What tears are like the wondering tears
Of that entranced embrace,
When out of desolate and divided years
Face meets beloved face?
What cry most exquisite of grief or bliss
The too full heart shall tell,
When the new-recovered kiss
Is the kiss of last farewell?

II

Isoult
O Tristram, is this true?
Is it thou I see
With my own eyes, clasp in my arms? I knew,
I knew that this must be.
Thou couldst not suffer so.
And I not feel the smart.
Far, far away. But oh.
How pale, my love, thou art!

Tristram
Tis I, Isoult, 'tis I
That thee enfold.
I have seen thee, my own life, and yet I die.
O for my strength of old!
O that thy love could heal
This wound that conquers me!
But the night is come, I feel.
And the last sun set for me.

Isoult
Tristram, 'twas I that healed thy hurt,
That old, fierce wound of Morolt's poisoned sword.
Stricken to death, pale, pale as now thou wert:
Yet was thy strength restored.
Have I forgot my skill?
This wound shall yet be healed.
Love shall be master still,
And Death again shall yield!

Tristram
Isoult, if Time could bring me back
That eve, that first eve, and that Irish shore.
Then should I fear not, no nor nothing lack.

And life were mine once more.
But now too late thou art come;
Too long we have dwelt apart;
I have pined in an alien home:
This new joy bursts my heart.

Isoult
Hark, Tristram, to the breaking sea!
So sounded the dim waves, at such an hour
On such an eve, when thy voice came to me
First in my father's tower.
I heard thy sad harp from the shore beneath,
It stirred my soul from sleep.
Then it was bliss to breathe;
But now, but now, I weep.

Tristram
Shipwrecked, without hope, without friend, alone
On a strange shore, stricken with pang on pang,
I stood sad-hearted by that tower unknown.
Yet soon for joy I sang.
For could I see thee and on death believe?
Ah, glad would I die to attain
The beat of my heart, that eve,
And the song in my mouth again!

Isoult
Young was I then and fair,
Thou too wast fair and young;
How comely the brown hair
Down on thy shoulder hung!
O Tristram, all grows dark as then it grew.
But still I see thee on that surge-beat shore;
Thou camest, and all was new
And changed for evermore.

Tristram
Isoult, dost thou regret?
Behold my wasted cheek,
With salt tears it is wet,
My arms how faint, how weak!

And thou, since that far day, what hast thou seen
Save strife, and tears, and failure, and dismay?
Had that hour never been.
Peace had been thine, this day.

Isoult

Look, Tristram, in my eyes!
My own love, I could feed
Life- well with miseries
So thou wert mine indeed.
Proud were the tears I wept;
That day, that hour I bless,
Nor would for peace accept
One single pain the less.

Tristram

Isoult, my heart is rent.
What pangs our bliss hath bought!
Only joy we meant.
Yet woe and wrong we have wrought.
I vowed a vow in the dark.
And thee, who wert mine, I gave
For a word's sake, to King Mark!
Words, words have digged our grave.

Isoult

Tristram, despite thy love,
King Mark had yet thine oath.
Ah, surely thy heart strove
How to be true to both.
Blame not thyself! for woe
'Twixt us was doomed to be.
One only thing I know;
Thou hast been true to me.

Tristram

Accurst be still that day,
When lightly I vowed the king
Whatever he might pray
Home to his hands I'd bring!
Thee, thee he asked! And I
Who never feared man's sword,
Yielded my life to a lie,
To save the truth of a word.

Isoult

Think not of that day, think
Of the day when our lips desired.
Unknowing, that cup to drink!
The cup with a charm was fired

From thee to beguile my love:
But now in my soul it must burn
For ever, nor turn, nor remove.

Till the sun in his course shall turn.

Tristram
Or ever that draught we drank,
Thy heart, Isoult, was mine,
My heart was thine. I thank
God's grace, no magic wine.
No purple drop distilled
By spells, no wizard art,
No charm, could have ever filled
With aught but thee my heart.

Isoult
When last we said farewell.
Remember how we dreamed
Wild love to have learned to quell;
Our hearts grown wise we deemed.
Tender, parted friends
We vowed to be; but the will
Of Love meant other ends.
Words fool us, Tristram, still.

Tristram
Not now, Isoult, not now!
I am thine while I have breath.
Words part us not, nor vow —
No, nor King Mark, but death.
I hold thee to my breast.
Our sins, our woes are past;
Thy lips were the first I prest,
Thou art mine, thou art mine at the last!

Isoult
O Tristram, all grows old.
Enfold me closer yet!
The night grows vast and cold.
And the dew on thy hair falls wet.
And never shall Time rebuild
The places of our delight;
Those towers and gardens are filled
With emptiness now, and night!

Tristram
Isoult, let it all be a dream.
Those days and those deeds, let them be
As the leaves that I cast on the stream
And that lived but to bring thee to me;
As the oak-leaves I broke from the bough

To float past thy window, and say-
That I waited thy coming — O now
Thou art come, let the world away!

Isoult
How dark is the strong waves' sound!
Tristram, they fill me with fear!
We two are but spent waves, drowned
In the coming of year upon year.
Long dead are our friends and our foes.
Old Rual, Brangian, all
That helped us, or wrought us woes;
And we, the last, we fall.

Tristram
God and his great saints guard
True friends that loved us well.
And all false foes be barred
In the fiery gates of hell.
But broken be all those towers.
And sunken be all those ships!
Shut out those old, dead hours;
Life, life, is on thy lips!

Isoult
Tristram, my soul is afraid!

Tristram
Isoult, Isoult, thy kiss!
To sorrow though I was made,
I die in bliss, in bliss.

Isoult
Tristram, my heart must break.
O leave me not in the grave
Of the dark world! Me too take!
Save me, O Tristram, save!

III

Calm, calm the moving waters all the night
On to that shore roll slow,
Fade into foam against the cliffs dim height.
And fall in a soft thunder, and upsurge
Forever out of unexhausted might.
Lifting their voice below
Tuned to no human dirge;

Nor from their majesty of music bend
To wail for beauty's end
Or towering spirit's most fiery overthrow;
Nor tarrieth the dawn, though she unveil
To weeping eyes their woe.
The dawn that doth not know
What the dark night hath wrought.
And over the far wave comes pacing pale.
Of all that she reveals regarding nought. —
But ere the dawn there comes a faltering tread;
Isoult, the young wife, stealing from her bed.
Sleepless with dread.
Creeps by still wall and blinded corridor.
Till from afar the salt scent of the air
Blows on her brow; and now
O what pale space beyond the open door
And what dim shadow strike her to despair
By keen degrees aware
That with the dawn her widowhood is there?

Is it wild envy or remorseful fear
Transfixes her young heart, unused to woe,
Crying to meet wrath, hatred, any foe.
Not silence drear!
Not to be vanquished so
By silence on the lips that were so dear!
Ah, sharpest stab! it is another face
That leans to Tristram's piteous embrace,
Another face she knows not, yet knows well,
Whose hands are clasped about his helpless head.
Propping it where it fell
In a vain tenderness,
But dead, — her great dream-hated rival dead,
Invulnerably dead,
Dead as her love, and cold.
And on her heart a grief heavy as stone is rolled.
She bows down, stricken in accusing pain,
And love, long-baffled, surges back again
Over her heart; she wails a shuddering cry,
While the tears blindly rain,
"I, I have killed him, I that loved him, I
That for his dear sake had been glad to die.
I loved him not enough, I could not keep
His heart, and yet I loved him, O how deep!
I cannot touch him. Will none set him free
From those, those other arms and give him me?
Alas, I may not vex him from that sleep.
He is thine in the end, thou proud one, he is thine,

Not mine, not mine!
I loved him not enough, I could not hold
My tongue from stabbing, and forsook him there.
I had not any care
To keep him from the darkness and the cold.
O all my wretched servants, where were ye?
Hath none in my house tended him but she?
Where are ye now? Can ye not hear my call?
Come hither, laggards all!
Nay, hush not so affrighted, nor so stare
Upon your lord; tis he!
Put out your torches, for the dawn grows clear.
And set me out within the hall a bier,
And wedding robes, the costliest that are
In all my house, prepare.
And lay upon the silks these princely dead.
And bid the sailors take that funeral bed
And set it in the ship, and put to sea.
And north to Cornwall steer.
Farewell, my lord, thy home is far from here.
Farewell, my great love, dead and doubly dear!
Carry him hence, proud queen, for he is thine.
Not mine, not mine, not mine! "

Within Tintagel walls King Mark awaits his queen.
The south wind blows, surely she comes to-day!
No light hath his eye seen
Since she is gone, no pleasure; he grows gray;
His knights apart make merry and wassail,
With dice and chessboard, hound at knee, they play;
But he sits solitary all the day,
Thinking of what hath been.
And now through all the castle rings a wail;
The king arises; all his knights are dumb;
The queen, the queen is come.
Not as she came of old,
Sweeping with gesture proud
To meet her wronged lord, royally arrayed,
And music ushered her, and tongues were stayed.
And all hearts beat, her beauty to behold;
But mute she comes and cold.
Borne on a bier, apparelled in a shroud.
Daisies about her sprinkled; and now bowed
Is her lord's head; and hushing upon all
Thoughts of sorrow fall,
As the snow softly, without any word;
And every breast is stirred
With wonder in its weeping;

For by her sleeping side,
In that long sleep no morning shall divide,
Is Tristram sleeping;
Tristram who wept farewell, and fled, and swore
That he would clasp his dear love never more,
And sailed far over sea
Far from his bliss and shame.
And dreamed to die at peace in Brittany
And to uncloud at last the glory of his name.
Yet lo, with fingers clasping both are come.
Come again home
In all men's sight, as when of old they came,
And Tristram led Isoult, another's bride.
True to his vow, but to his heart untrue,
And silver trumpets blew
To greet them stepping o'er the flower-strewn floor,
And King Mark smiled upon them, and men cried
On Tristram's name anew,
Tristram, the king's strong champion and great pride.

Silently gazing long
On them that wrought him wrong,
Still stands the stricken king, and to his eyes
Such tears as old men weep, yet shed not, rise:
Lifting his head at last, as from a trance, he sighs.
"Beautiful ever, O Isoult, wast thou,
And beautiful art thou now.
Though never again shall I, reproaching thee.
Make thy proud head more beautiful to me;
But this is the last reproach, and this the last
Forgiveness that thou hast.
Lost is the lost, Isoult, and past the past!
O Tristram, no more shalt thou need to hide
Thy thought from my thought, sitting at my side,
Nor need to wrestle sore
With thy great love and with thy fixèd oath.
For now Death leaves thee loyal unto both.
Even as thou wouldst have been, for evermore.
Now, after all thy pain, thy brow looks glad;
But I lack all things that I ever had.
My wife, my friend, yea, even my jealous rage;
And empty is the house of my old age.
Behold, I have laboured all my days to part
These two, that were the dearest to my heart.
Isoult, I would have fenced thee from men's sight,
My treasure, that I found so very fair.
The treasure I had taken with a snare:
To keep thee mine, this was my life's delight.

And now the end is come, alone I stand,
And the hand that lies in thine is not my hand."

AMASIS

I

"O King Amasis, hail!
News from thy friend, the King Polycrates!
My oars have never rested on the seas
From Samos, nor on land my horse's hoofs,
Till I might tell my tale."
Sais, the sacred city, basked her roofs
And gardens whispering in the western light;
Men thronged abroad to taste the coming cool of night:
Only the palace closed
Unechoing courts, where by the lake reposed,
Wide-eyed, the enthroned shapes of Memphian deities;
And King Amasis in the cloistered shade.
That guards them, of a giant colonnade.
Paced musing; there he pondered mysteries
That are the veils of truth;
For mid those gods of grave, ignoring smile
Large auguries he spelled,
Forgot the spears, the tumults of his youth,
And strangled Apries, and the reddened Nile.
Now turning, he beheld,
Half in a golden shadow and half touched with flame,
The white-robed stranger from the Grecian isle.
And heard pronounced his name.

II

"Welcome from Samos, friend!
Good news, I think, thou bearest in thy mien,"
The king spoke welcoming with voice serene.
"How is it with Polycrates, thy lord?
Peace on his name attend!
Would he were here in Egypt, and his sword
Could sheathe, and we at god-like ease discourse
Of counsel no ignoble needs enforce.
And take august regale
Of wisdom from the Powers whose purpose cannot fail.
I, too, O man of Samos, bred to war,
Passed youth, passed manhood, in a life of blood;

But many victories bring the heart no certain good.
Would that he too might tease his fate no more.
And I might see his face
In presence of my land's ancestral Powers, —
See, from their countenance, what a grandeur beams!
Thou know'st I love thy race;
Bright wits ye have, skill in adventurous schemes;
But deeper life is ours:
Fed by these springs, your strength might bless the world. But lo!
The light begins to fade from the high towers.
Thy errand let me know."

III

"Thus saith Polycrates:
The counsel which thou wrotest me is well;
For, seeing how full crops my granaries swell,
How all winds waft me to prosperity.
How I gain all with ease,
And my raised banner pledges victory,
Thou didst advise me cast away what most
Brought pleasure to my eyes and seemed of rarest cost.
And after heavy thought
I chose the ring which Theodorus wrought.
My famous emerald, where young Phaethon
Shoots headlong with pale limbs through glowing air,
While green waves from beneath toss white drops to his hair.
A long time, very loth, I gazed thereon;
For this cause, thought I, men most envy me;
I took a ship, and fifty beating oars
Bore me far out to sea:
I stood upon the poop — but wherefore tell
What now is rumoured round all Asian shores?
Say only I did well.
Who the world's envy treasured yet in deep waves drowned.
Homeward I came, and mourned within my doors
Three days, nor solace found."

IV

Amasis without word
Listens, dark-browed: the Samian speaks anew:
"Let not the king this thing so deeply rue;
Truly the gem was of imperial price,
Nay even, men averred,
Coveted more than wealthy satrapies.

Nor twenty talents could its loss redeem:
Yet hear! the Gods are more benignant than men dream.
Thus saith my lord: The moon
Not once had waned, when as I sat at noon
Within my palace court above the Lydian bay,
They led before me with much wondering noise
A fisherman; between two staggering boys
Slung heavily a fish he brought, that day
Caught in his bursting net,
A royal fish for royal destiny!
I marvelled; but amaze broke deeper yet
To recognise Heaven's hand,
When from its cloven belly (surely high
In that large grace I stand)
Dazzled my eyes with light, my heart with joy, the ring
Restored! — Why rendest thou thy robe, and why
Lamentest thou, O king? "

V

"O lamentable news!"
Amasis cried; "now have the Gods indeed
Doom on thy head, Polycrates, decreed!
I feared already, when I heard thy joy
Must need stoop down to choose
For sacrifice, loss of a shining toy.
Searching the suburbs only of content,
Not thy heart's home: what God this blindness on thee sent?
Gone was thy ring; yet how
Was thy soul cleared, or thou more greatly thou?
Were vain things vainer, or the dear more dear?
Hast thou, bent gazing o'er thy child asleep.
Thoughts springing, tender as new leaves? Deep, deep,
Deep as thy inmost hope, as thy most sacred fear,
Thou shouldst have sought the pain
That changes earth's wide aspect in an hour.
Heaved by abysmal throes!
Ah, then our pleasant refuges are vain;
Yet, thrilled, the soul assembles all her power.
And cleared by peril glows,
Seeing immortal hosts arrayed upon her side!
Blind man, the scornful Gods thy offering slight:
My fears are certified."

VI

Swift are the thoughts of fear.
But Fate at will rides swifter far; and lo!
Even as Amasis bows to boded woe.
Even as his robe, with a sad cry, he rends.
The accomplishment is here.
The sun that from the Egyptian plain descends,
Blessing with holier shade
Those strange gods dreaming throned by the vast colonnade,
Burns o'er the northern sea.
Firing the peak of Asian Mycale,
Firing a cross raised on the mountain side!
Folycrates the Fortunate hangs there:
The false Oroetes hath him in a snare;
Now with his quivering limbs his soul is crucified;
And in his last hour first
He tastes the extremity of loss; he burns
With ecstasy of thirst;
Nought recks he even of his dearest now,
Moaning for breath; no pity he discerns
On the dark Persian's brow:
Grave on his milk-white horse, in silks of Sidon shawled.
The Satrap smiles, and on his finger turns
The all-envied emerald.

ORPHEUS IN THRACE

I

Dear is the newly won,
But O far dearer the forever lost!
He that at utmost cost
His utmost deed hath done
The lost one to recover, and in vain,
What shall his heart, his anguished heart, sustain?
Not the warm and youthful sun.
Flowers breathing on the bough,
Nor a voice, nor music now —
Touches of joy, more hard to bear than pain!
These charm not where he is, but only there
Where she is gone, who took with her delight.
Peace, and all things fair.
And left the whole world bare.
And O, what far well's fountain shall requite
Him who hath drunk so deeply of despair?

Orpheus on a stone-strewn slope

High amid the hills of Thrace
Sets to the bleak North his face.
He, a traveller from hope,
As a bird whose mate is stricken
Flies and flies o'er ocean foam
Nor endures to seek a home,
Seeks a land where no leaves quicken.
Where from gorges to the plain
Iron-tongued the torrent roars
Into troubled streams that strain
Eddying under barren shores;
Where thronged ridges darkly rise.
Shouldering the storms that sweep
Through the winter-loaded skies.
When far up in heavens asleep
For an hour the clouds unclose: —
Throned in peace beyond the bourne
Of their moving vapours torn.
Glimmer the majestic snows.
Whence an eagle slowly sails
O'er the solitary vales.
Such to Orpheus' pilgrim eyes
The unreached far mountains rise.
"Come," he groans, "you storms, and scourge me,
Dull these inward pangs that urge me
Ever into new despair.
Make my flesh endure as steel,
Let me now the utmost feel,
Bring me news of things that bear —
Frozen torrents, naked trees
That abjure the summer's breeze, —
Keen upon this body fall!
O let me feel your fiercest sting or feel no more at all!"

His hand, half-conscious, straying
Over the well-loved lyre.
Strikes; frail notes obeying
Sadly in air expire.
Wingless they falter forth.
As the pale large plumes of snow
From the dim cloud-curdling North,
Unwilling and soft and slow.
That fall on the hands and the hair
Of Orpheus unheeded, and die.
As out of his heart's despair
He speaks to his lyre: "Ah, why
Would I stir thee from silence now.
When silence is far the best?

As of old I touch thee, but thou
Unwillingly answerest.
Ah, marvellous once was thy power
In the marvellous days of old!
I touched thee, and all hearts heard,
And the snake had no thought to devour.
And the shy fawn stayed and was bold.
And the panther crept near in desire;
And the toppling Symplegades hung
To hearken thy strings as I sung,
And Argo glanced through like a bird,
Like a swallow, to hear thee, my lyre!
And the soul of the dragon was stirred.
Till his vast coil slowly stooped
From the tree where the Fleece glimmered gold,
And his ageless eyelids drooped.
And his strength sank, fold by fold;
And only the dim leaves heard,
As we stept o'er his coils that were cold.
Mighty wast thou indeed;
But O, in my utmost need.
My heart thou couldst not quell,
My heart that loved too well!
I turned on the brink of the light;
Her hand hung fast in my own;
I was sure as a God in my might;
I gazed; she grew pale, she was flown.
Then the dawn turned back to the night.
And I stood in the world alone.
Eurydice, could I have loved thee less
I had won thee lightly again.
But my great joy wrought my wretchedness,
And thee, whom I love, I have slain."

II

What lights are these that dance,
Like fire-flies clustering on the dusk hillside,
Mingle and then divide,
Swerve and again advance.
Peopling the shadows thick, till Rhodope
Seems rocking all her towering pines in glee?
Maenads of exultant glance,
Thracian maidens, Thracian dames.
Toss these perilous fair flames.
Soon their full tresses roll from neck to knee,
Swift as a dark shower in the sunset poured;

Soon panting bosoms from rent robes shine bare!
Thoughts leap in accord,
Bright as an unsheathed sword,
Tumultuously free, and mad to dare;
And loud they cry on Bacchus, their wild lord.

O can cheeks of white and red.
Lips that love made tremble often.
Eyes an infant's tears can soften,
Alter with a change so dread?
Yea, a deep fire craving fuel,
Like the dungeoned fires of Earth,
Pants from secresy for birth,
Careless if its way be cruel.
While from tempest faint they stand,
Orpheus mid their riot strays,
Silent halts with listless hand
And with sorrow-sunken gaze.
"Who is this?" in wrath they cry,
"Spectre sprung to mock our glee!
Woe to this pale face, for he
Joins our mirth or he shall die!" —
Singer, touch thy magic lyre!
Thou couldst stay them soft and still.
Tamed and gentle, to thy will.
Ah, in grief is no desire.
Grief in stony' bonds hath bound him.
And these bright forms that surround him
With high torches menacing
And light spears in restless ring,
Seem his own thoughts raging, seem
Furies of embodied dream.
Furies whom 'tis vain to flee.
Alas, he hath for shield and sword
Only one defenceless word,
"Eurydice, Eurydice!"
To piercing wound and branding flame
He answers with that piteous name
The world now echoes back alone.
"Eurydice!" his soul flies forth in that beloved moan.

Alas, that the hand should deflower
The treasure the heart loves best,
That the will of an alien power
Should blindly the soul have possest!
Proudly our own great woe
We accomplish, and laugh to have done.
Then strength passes from us; we know,

And we hide our heads from the sun.
Behold, as the dawn-flushed air
Glimmers on peak and vale,
To the pines on the upland bare
Come shadowy forms and pale;
Stealing, maiden and mother,
By single paths of dread.
And wondering each at the other
Bend over the piteous dead.
And touching those rent limbs, cry,
With kisses kneeling low,
In sad affrighted moan,
"It was not I!" "Nor I!"
What evil God blinded us so
To wound our beloved, our delight?
For our dancing thou hadst not a song,
And now we have none for thy wrong.
Though thy lyre could charm honey from stone.
Yet we pitied not thee, our delight!
Nay, thee who couldst heal us alone
In our grief, at whose magical boon
Peace brooded a dove o'er our pain.
And our hearts with the sun and the moon
Were at peace, that shall be not again.
Nor our hope with the spring be in tune;
Thee, thee, even thee, have we slain!
Woe for the world, woe!
In cherishing fair snow
Let us bury thee whom we marred.
With the lyre that our flame hath charred.
Gentle wast thou as a flower,
But careless as thunder were we;
And our tears, that should be as a shower
To raise and to foster thee,
Drop vainly, and past is our power
With that blindness and fury and glee.
Yea, the solace we wanted not then in our mirth
From our helpless sorrow is taken;
And forever untuned is the beautiful earth,
And the home of our hearts is forsaken.

AUTUMN MOONRISE

Lamp that risest lone
From thy secret place,
Like a sleeper's face,

Charged with thoughts unknown,

Strange thoughts, unexpressed
In thy brightening beam.
Strangeness more than dream
Upon earth e'er guessed!

Strange thou gleam'st as some
Eastern marble old.
Scrawled with runes that hold
Histories, yet are dumb.

But thy viewless hand
Out of whelming night
Waves the woods to light.
Summons up the land!

Sea, that merged in sky,
To its far bound shines;
And thy touch defines
Our infinity.

Now the murmuring coast
Glistens; rocks are there;
And what most was bare
Thou enrichest most.

Far through granite caves
Diving glide thy beams,
Till the dark roof gleams
Laced with hovering waves;

O'er the white walls glide,
Through the lattice creep.
Where the lovers sleep.
Bridegroom by his bride.

Soft their wakened eyes
From a deep bliss gaze
On those marvellous rays
New from Paradise.

In the self-same hour,
Whitening Russian plains,
On sad exile trains
Thou hast also power.

No more kindly gloom

Veils from them despair:
Near and clear and bare
They behold their doom.

Bowed, they see their own
Shadows on the snow,
And the way they go,
Endlessly alone:

Aching, chained, footsore.
Through the waste they wind.
All their joy behind.
Nought but grief before.

O thou sleeper's face
Whence hast thou this gift
So much to uplift.
And so much to abase?

Lovers' happier dream,
Exiles' heavier pain,
Thou on each dost rain
Beam on radiant beam.

Changed in thy control.
Though no leaf hath stirred,
Though no breath was heard
Lie both world and souL

THE BELFRY OF BRUGES

Keen comes the dizzy air
In one tumultuous breath.
The tower to heaven lies bare;
Dumb stir the streets beneath.

Immeasurable sky
Domes upward from the dim
Round land, the astonished eye
Supposes the world's rim.

And through the sea of space
Winds drive the furious cloud
Silent in endless race;
And the tower rocks aloud.

Mine eye now wanders wide,
My thought now quickens keen.
O cities, far descried,
What ravage have you seen

Of an enkindled world?
Homes blazing and hearths bare;
Of hosts tyrannic hurled
On pale ranks of despair,

Who fed with warm proud blood
The cause unquenchable,
For which your heroes stood,
For which our Sidney fell;

Sidney, whose starry fame.
Mirrored in noble song,
Shines, all our sloth to shame.
And arms us against wrong;

Bright star, that seems to burn
Over yon English shore,
Whither my feet return.
And my thoughts run before;

Run with this rumour brought
By the wild wind's alarms,
Dark sounds with battle fraught,
Menace of distant arms.

O menace harsh, but vain!
For what can peril do
But search our souls again
To sift and find the true?

Prove if the sap of old
Shoots yet from the old seed,
If faith be still unsold,
If truth be truth indeed?

Welcome the blast that shakes
The wall wherein we have lain
Slumbering, our heart awakes
And rends the prison chain.

Turn we from prosperous toys
And the dull name of ease;
Rather than tarnished joys

Face we the angry seas!

Or, if old age infirm
Be in our veins congealed.
Bow we to Time, our term
Fulfilled, and proudly yield.

Not each to each we are made,
Not each to each we fall,
But every true part played
Quickens the heart of all

That feeds and moves and fires
The many-peopled lands.
And in our languor tires
But in our strength expands.

For forward-gazing eyes
Fate shall no terror keep.
She in our own breast lies:
Now let her wake from sleep!

Laurence Binyon – A Short Biography

Robert Laurence Binyon, CH, was born on August 10th, 1869 in Lancaster in Lancashire, England to Quaker parents, Frederick Binyon and Mary Dockray.

He studied at St Paul's School, London before enrolling at Trinity College, Oxford, to read classics.

Binyon's first published work was Persephone in 1890. Whilst only a few pages in length it certainly illustrated the talents that Binyon would develop as a poet even though he continued to advance multiple career opportunities.

Immediately after graduating in 1893, Binyon started work at the British Museum for the Department of Printed Books, writing catalogues for the museum and art monographs for himself. As well as being one of England's best poets he was also renowned for his knowledge of various arts particularly with regard to Japan and Persia.

His first poetry book Lyric Poems was published in 1894.

In 1895 his first art book, Dutch Etchers of the Seventeenth Century, was published and, that same year, Binyon moved into the Museum's Department of Prints and Drawings.

Whilst Binyon became known to a wide audience as a poet his output was not prodigious. In 1898, Porphyrion & Other Poems was published followed by Odes (1901) and The Death of Adam & Other Poems (1904).

That same year, 1904, Binyon married the historian Cicely Margaret Powell. The union was to produce three daughters.

In the early years of the 20th Century Binyon was a regular patron of the Wiener Cafe of London together with fellow artists and intellectuals; Ezra Pound, Sir William Rothenstein, Walter Sickert, Charles Ricketts, Lucien Pissarro and Edmund Dulac.

His poetic work continued despite the demands of the British Museum and his other interests. London Visions was published in 1908 followed by England & Other Poems in 1909.

His work at the British Museum ensured promotions were a frequent occurrence for Binyon. In 1909, he became its Assistant Keeper, and in 1913 he was made the Keeper of the new Sub-Department of Oriental Prints and Drawings.

It was also at this time that he played a crucial role in the formation of Modernism in London by introducing young Imagist poets such as Ezra Pound, Richard Aldington and H.D. (Hilda Doolittle) to East Asian visual art and literature.

Many of Binyon's books produced while at the Museum were influenced by his own sensibilities as a poet, although some are clearly works of plain scholarship, such as his four volume catalogue of all the Museum's English drawings, and his seminal catalogue of Chinese and Japanese prints.

Binyon's poetic reputation before the war, although built on several slim volumes, was such that, on the death of the Poet Laureate Alfred Austin in 1913, Binyon was among the names considered as his likely successor. It was quite a field. Among the other illustrious contenders were Thomas Hardy, John Masefield and Rudyard Kipling; however the post was awarded to Robert Bridges.

Moved and shaken by the onset of the World War I and its military tactics of young men slaughtered to hold or gain a few yards of shell-shocked mud as the British Expeditionary Force began its campaign Binyon wrote his seminal poem For the Fallen, with its Ode of Remembrance (the third and fourth or simply the fourth stanza of the poem). The poem was published by The Times newspaper on September 21st, when public feeling was shaken by the recent Battle of Marne. It became an instant classic, turning moments of great loss into a National and human tribute.

Today, For the Fallen, is often recited at Remembrance Sunday services as well as being an integral part of Anzac Day services in Australia and New Zealand and of November 11th Remembrance Day services in Canada. The "Ode of Remembrance" is now acknowledged as a tribute to all casualties of war, irrespective of nation.

In 1915, despite being too old to enlist, Binyon volunteered at a British hospital for French soldiers, the Hôpital Temporaire d'Arc-en-Barrois, Haute-Marne, France, working for a short time as a hospital orderly.

He returned there in the summer of 1916 and took care of soldiers taken in from the Verdun battlefield. He wrote about his experiences in For Dauntless France (1918) and his poems, "Fetching the Wounded" and "The Distant Guns", were inspired by his hospital service.

After the war, he returned to the British Museum and wrote numerous books on art; especially on William Blake, Persian and Japanese art. His work on ancient Japanese and Chinese cultures offered inspiration that inspired many, among them the poets Ezra Pound and W. B. Yeats. His work on Blake and his followers kept alive the then nearly-forgotten memory of the work of Samuel Palmer. Binyon's spectrum of interests continued the traditional interest of British visionary Romanticism in the rich strangeness of Mediterranean and Oriental cultures.

In 1931, his two volume Collected Poems appeared and by 1932, Binyon was promoted to the post of Keeper of the Prints and Drawings Department. The following year, 1933, he retired from the British Museum. He went to live in the country at Westridge Green, near Streatley but continued writing poetry.

In 1933–1934, Binyon was appointed Norton Professor of Poetry at Harvard University. He delivered a series of lectures on The Spirit of Man in Asian Art, which were published in 1935.

Binyon continued his academic work: in May, 1939 he gave the prestigious Romanes Lecture in Oxford on Art and Freedom, and in 1940 he was appointed the Byron Professor of English Literature at the University of Athens. He worked there until forced to leave by the German invasion of Greece in April, 1941.

Binyon had been friends with Ezra Pound for a long time, and in the 1930s the two became especially close; Pound affectionately called him "BinBin", and he assisted Binyon with his translation of Dante.

Between 1933 and 1943, Binyon published his acclaimed translation of Dante's Divine Comedy in an English version of terza rima, made with some editorial assistance by Ezra Pound. It was acknowledged for many decades as *the* popular translation for Dante readers.

During the horrors of the Second World War Binyon wrote a poem that many claim as to be a masterpiece 'The Burning of the Leaves', puts in print his lines on the London Blitz.

At his death Binyon was working on a major three-part Arthurian trilogy, the first part of which was published after his death as The Madness of Merlin (1947).

Robert Laurence Binyon died in Dunedin Nursing Home, Bath Road, Reading, on March 10th, 1943 after undergoing an operation. A funeral service was held at Trinity College Chapel, Oxford, on March 13th, 1943.

Binyon's ashes were scattered at St. Mary's Church, Aldworth.

On November 11th, 1985, Binyon was among sixteen poets of the Great War commemorated on a slate stone unveiled in Westminster Abbey's Poets' Corner. The inscription on the stone quotes a fellow Great War poet, Wilfred Owen. It reads: "My subject is War, and the pity of War. The Poetry is in the pity."

Laurence Binyon – A Concise Bibliography

Poems and Verse

Persephone (1890)
Lyric Poems (1894)
The Praise of Life (1896)
Porphyrion & Other Poems (1898)
Odes (1901)
Death of Adam & Other Poems (1904)
Penthesilea (1905)
London Visions (1908)
England & Other Poems (1909)
Auguries (1913)
For The Fallen (The Times, September 21st, 1914)
The Winnowing Fan (1914)
The Anvil (1916)
The Cause (1917)
The New World: Poems (1918)
The Secret: Sixty Poems (1920)
The Idols (1928)
Collected Poems Vol I: London Visions, Narrative Poems, Translations (1931)
Collected Poems Vol II: Lyrical Poems (1931)
The North Star & Other Poems (1941)
The Burning of the Leaves & Other Poems (1944)
The Madness of Merlin (1947)

Poems Set to Music

In 1915 Cyril Rootham set "For the Fallen" for chorus and orchestra, first performed in 1919 by the Cambridge University Musical Society conducted by the composer.

Edward Elgar set to music "The Fourth of August", "To Women", and "For the Fallen", as The Spirit of England, Op. 80, for tenor or soprano solo, chorus and orchestra (1917).

English Arts and Myth

Dutch Etchers of the Seventeenth Century (1895), Binyon's first book on painting
John Crone and John Sell Cotman (1897)
William Blake: Being all his Woodcuts Photographically Reproduced in Facsimile (1902)
English Poetry in its relation to painting and the other arts (1918)
Drawings and Engravings of William Blake (1922)
Arthur: A Tragedy (1923)
The Followers of William Blake (1925)
The Engraved Designs of William Blake (1926)
Landscape in English Art and Poetry (1931)
English Watercolours (1933)
Gerard Hopkins and his influence (1939)
Art and freedom. (The Romanes lecture, delivered 25 May 1939). Oxford: The Clarendon press, (1939)

Japanese and Persian Arts

Painting in the Far East (1908)
Japanese Art (1909)
Flight of the Dragon (1911)
The Court Painters of the Grand Moguls (1921)
Japanese Colour Prints (1923)
The Poems of Nizami (1928) (Translation)
Persian Miniature Painting (1933)
The Spirit of Man in Asian Art (1936)
Autobiography[edit]
For Dauntless France (1918) (War memoir)

Biography
Botticelli (1913)
Akbar (1932)

Stage Plays
Brief Candles A verse-drama about the decision of Richard III to dispatch his two nephews
Paris and Œnone. A Tragedy in One Act (1906)
Godstow Nunnery: Play
Boadicea; A Play in eight Scenes
Attila: A Tragedy in Four Acts (1907)
Ayuli: A Play in three Acts and an Epilogue
Sophro the Wise: A Play for Children
(Most of the above were written for John Masefield's theatre).